I0440189

My First Book about the Alphabet of Butterflies & Moths

Amazing Animal Books Children's Picture Books

By Molly Davidson

Mendon Cottage Books

JD-Biz Publishing

Download Free Books!
http://MendonCottageBooks.com

All Rights Reserved.

No part of this publication may be reproduced in any form or by any means, including scanning, photocopying, or otherwise without prior written permission from JD-Biz Corp and http://AmazingAnimalBooks.com.
Copyright © 2016

All Images Licensed by Fotolia, Pixabay, and 123RF

Read More Amazing Animal Books

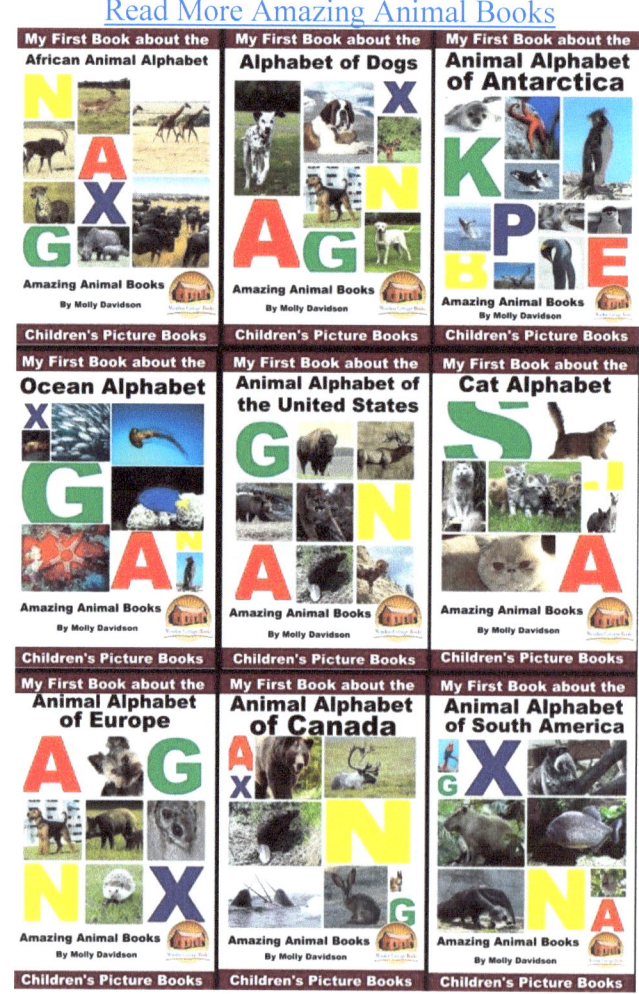

Purchase at Amazon.com

Download Free Books!
http://MendonCottageBooks.com

Introduction

There are over 20,000 different species of butterflies in the World and over 130,000 different species of moths!

Butterflies are very helpful to the environment, because they help pollinate many flowers and caterpillars are a main food source for birds.

Butterflies have a very interesting life cycle.

They first start out as tiny eggs, laid on a leaf.

Next, they hatch as a caterpillar. They don't stay caterpillars for very long and all they do is eat.

Third, after the caterpillar is as big as it can be, it forms a chrysalis around its self. Inside it begins changing into a butterfly.

The last stage is when the butterfly breaks out of the chrysalis and can begin flying, pollinating, and mating.

 **is for an American Snout Butterfly.**

American snout butterflies live in the southern United States during the summer and migrate to Mexico and Argentina in the winter.

Their wingspan is about 2 inches across.

 **is for a Blue Morpho Butterfly.**

Blue morpho butterflies have teeny tiny scales on the back of their wings which reflect light, this is why they are such a bright blue color.

They are large butterflies with a wingspan of up to 8 inches.

C is for a Chequered Skipper Butterfly.

Chequered skipper butterflies live in Spain, the UK, Asia, Japan, Canada, and the northern U.S.

The boys are a little smaller than the girls.

In North America they're called the Arctic Skipper.

D is for a Doris Longwing Butterfly.

Doris longwing butterflies like to be in the sun and live in Bolivia north to Mexico.

They live for about 9 months, which is long for a rainforest butterfly.

E is for an European Peacock Butterfly.

European peacock butterflies are a very common butterfly seen all over Europe, except in the colder northern region.

They hibernate from September to the beginning of April, in dark places; like tree trunks, barns, and animal burrows.

F is for a Figure of Eighty Moth.

Figure of eighty moths have white markings on their wings that look like the number 80, this is where they get their name from.

They are found mostly in England and Whales.

G is a Garden Tiger Moth.

Garden tiger moths love wet places; this is why they live in gardens and river valleys.

 **is for a High Brown Fritillary.**

High brown fritillaries are on the endangered list, they used to fly all over England and Whales, now there are only a few groups left.

They have a wingspan of about 2 1/2 inches.

I is for an Io Moth.

Io moths have two large black dots on the bottom of their wings, which trick predators into thinking they are eyes.

Young io moth caterpillars follow each other in a long line from leaf to leaf.

J is for a Julia Butterfly.

The Julia butterfly lives near the equator from Texas to Brazil.

They're very fast fliers and are kept in many butterfly houses because they are active during the day.

 **is for a Karner Blue Butterfly.**

Karner blue butterflies are a small endangered butterfly that lives around the Great Lakes.

They only like to fly when the temperature is between 76°F and 96°F.

Girls are lay up to 83 eggs at one time.

L is for a Luna Moth.

Luna moths only fly at night in the spring and summer.

They are a large moth with a wingspan of up to 4 1/2 inches.

 **is for a Monarch.**

Monarchs are a beautiful orange color which tells predators that they are poisonous.

Many make a 3,000 mile journey to migrate from Canada to Mexico every winter.

 **is for a Northern Brown Argus.**

Velela © <u>Wikimedia Commons</u>

Northern Brown Argus have a small white or brown dot on the top of their upperwing.

They fly low to the ground, under flowers and through the grass.

 **is for an Owly Sulphur.**

Owly sulphur butterflies are a rare butterfly seen only in central Europe.

They have a one inch black, hairy body with a wingspan of about 2 inches.

They can live for up to 2 years.

P is for a Painted Lady Butterfly.

Painted ladies migrate in huge groups from Northern Africa in the winter to Britain and Ireland in the summer.

The caterpillars love to eat thistles.

 **is for Queen Alexandra's Birdwing.**

Queen Alexandra's butterfly is the largest butterfly in the World, with a wingspan of almost 10 inches!

is for a Red Admiral Butterfly.

Red admiral butterflies are seen all over Europe from tiny villages on the coast to the top of mountains.

They like to eat fruit and flowering ivy plants.

S is for a Small White Butterfly.

Small white butterflies are also called small cabbage white butterflies and are found almost everywhere in the World, except in cold areas.

Cabbage worms (the caterpillars of a small white butterfly) are a pest to farmers, because they eat all their mustard plants.

T is for a Tiger Swallowtail.

Tiger swallowtails are found in the eastern United States.

The girls are bigger than the boys and their wingspan can be from 3 - 5 1/2 inches.

U is for an Ulysses Butterfly.

Willem Van Aken, CSIRO ©Wikimedia Commons

Ulysses butterflies are large, with a wingspan of up to 4 inches.

They live in Australia and New Guinea.

Their wings have tiny scales which reflect light, making them a shiny blue color.

 **is for a Viceroy Butterfly.**

Viceroy butterflies have the same wing pattern as a Monarch, this is to trick their predators into thinking they are poisonous, even when they aren't.

W is for a Western Pygmy Blue Butterfly.

Anne Toal © <u>Wikimedia Commons</u>

A western pygmy blue butterfly is the smallest butterfly in the United States with a wingspan of less than 1/2 an inch.

 **is for Xerces Blue Butterfly.**

Brianwray26 © <u>Wikimedia Commons</u>

Xerces blue butterflies were the first known butterfly to become extinct in America.

They lived along the coast of California and the last living butterfly was seen in 1943.

 **is for Yellow Belle Moth.**

Ben Sale © <u>Wikimedia Commons</u>

Yellow belle moths can be found in south west Europe and North America.

They are a small moth with a wingspan from 1 - 1 1/2 inches.

Z is for Zebra Swallowtail Butterfly.

Zebra swallowtail butterflies lay up to 4 batches, called broods, of eggs per year.

They are the state butterfly of Tennessee.

They are easy to see due to their black and white stripes, which look like a zebra.

Conclusion

I hope you have enjoyed reading about many amazing butterflies.

One more fact, many butterflies taste flowers with sensors on their feet.

Download Free Books!

http://MendonCottageBooks.com

Purchase at Amazon.com
Website http://AmazingAnimalBooks.com

Our books are available at

1. Amazon.com

2. Barnes and Noble

3. Itunes

4. Kobo

5. Smashwords

6. Google Play Books

Download Free Books!
http://MendonCottageBooks.com

Publisher

JD-Biz Corp

P O Box 374

Mendon, Utah 84325

http://www.jd-biz.com/

www.ingramcontent.com/pod-product-compliance
Lightning Source LLC
Chambersburg PA
CBHW050848290526
45792CB00002B/572